CONTENTS

'Until he extends the circle of his compassion to all living things,

man himself, will not find Peace.'

(Albert Schweitzer)

This book is dedicated to Hope and my father, Richard ...
I miss you both so much ...

... and for my sons, Zachary, Samuel and Joseph
...You are all my heroes ...

♡ Momma

'I would rather be amongst forest animals and the sounds of nature,
than amongst city traffic and the noise of man.'

(Anthony Douglas Williams)

IN APPRECIATION...

The story of Hope takes place during one of the most emotional periods of my life. January 2012 began with my youngest son, Marine Cpl Taylor and his Military Working Dogs, IDD's Sgt Wren and Sgt Thor, in the middle of their tour of duty, in Afghanistan, the Southern Helmand Province, Kajaki District, probably one of the most deadly and dangerous of places on this earth.

So, late May 2012 brought great anticipation for me, as we would be welcoming home Golf Battery and the IDD's. My stressful, sleepless nights might finally come to an end upon their arrival. They came home with little fanfare and without two of their 'brother's in arms' who had been lost while serving 'over there' ... They were home now ... the healing could begin.

I was also anticipating the arrival of the Spring fawns to the forest and meadow, behind my house ~ such a happy and rejuvenating time of year ... little did I realize, my sleepless nights would not be over ...

So how does one say thank you, when mere words cannot express what is in your heart? I thank God for His Grace and Mercy in bringing our Joey safely home. I also thank Him for the bittersweet experience of Hope ... She was everything good; innocence, beauty, courage and love ... He opened my eyes to the dire needs of every one of us; compassion and kindness ... this world is full of hatred and cruelty to animals and to each other. My wish is that we would all strive to help the helpless and defend the defenseless ... "Compassion" ~ concern for the suffering ... Because all are precious in His sight ...

With that being said, let me just say a quiet but very heartfelt thank you, to my family and friends, for your prayers, love and support, and putting up with my tears and tirades ... to Tana Jo Ryan and Brandi Duran-Starr for helping me try to rescue Hope and get her to safety

... to Tana, also for the precious iconic photo of Hope taken from your bedroom window ~ I treasure it ... to my mom, Shirley Graham, for walking every step of this sad journey with me ... to my friend Elaine Camyn, for scavenging the ground for pears and apples and making sure Hope had food and water in my absence ... to Beth Amick Spears, Dory McIsaac and Debby Hill for your knowledge, expertise and support ... to my friend Mary Kivle for your grammar skills and encouraging chats ... to Pip Wallace at FriesenPress, for befriending me and keeping me focused throughout ~ you've been a Godsend ... to the designers and editors at FriesenPress for dealing with my use, misuse and overuse of ellipses and commas ... to my sister Betsy Miranda for introducing me to Sister Laura, and to Sister Laura for the use of your beautiful poem 'November Rain' ... to the rescuers and rehabbers everywhere for your tireless, difficult work helping lost, orphaned, injured and abused animals ~ you are Earth Angels ... to my husband Alan (Papa Owl), for allowing me to spend more money on food for all my little critters, than I do for ourselves and for tolerating an absent, emotional wreck of a wife ... to my boys, Zachary, Samuel and Joseph for loving and supporting me and graciously listening to all my sad stories, I love you all, so much and am so proud of the men you have become ... and to my little sweetheart Addy, for wiping away my tears for "our hurt little baby", and for your innocent understanding, sweet nature and love ... always when I needed it most ...

This journey would not have been possible, if not for all of you ... a very heartfelt Thank You ... and may God Bless you all ...

PREFACE

This is the true story of a gravely injured, three week old white-tailed fawn that I named "Hope", and her faithful family. I had named her "Hope" because I hoped she could survive our sometimes callous and cruel world.

By writing Hope's story, I am attempting to bring an awareness to the general population, that our deeds and actions can directly and adversely affect the wildlife that try to live peacefully among us. I fully understand there is a "circle of life" and that nature must take its course, but often times wildlife is injured and orphaned by humans, which dramatically shortens their lifespan. Over the years, I have seen far too many injuries to these gentle, vulnerable creatures that, for the most part, have been caused by man - intentionally or unintentionally - by means of vehicles, traps, snares, bullets, arrows, cyclone fencing and scrapped barbed wire, to name a few. So many of these injuries could have been avoided. I feel it is always important to help an animal in need, and especially so, when the suffering is a result of human error or intrusion ~ it's really just a matter of respect for life and one another.

If just one fawns' life is saved or changed because of Hope's story, then her passing, though tragic and heartbreaking, will not have been in vain.

This is her journey ...

"Think occasionally of the suffering ... of which you spare yourself the sight."

(Albert Schweitzer)

SPRING ...

I'm not exactly sure of the date, but it was late in June of 2012. It was a beautiful, late spring morning, so I was headed out to mow. Each time, I made a pass by the tall, grassy meadow behind my old apple tree in full bloom, I could swear that I was being watched. You know that feeling ... So I waited patiently to see just who might my little "visitor" be. It wasn't long till she appeared: a tiny, nervous, adorable fawn covered in hundreds of bright white speckles. She leaped out of the tall grass and onto my path. Being somewhat startled, she froze in her tracks and stared right at me, and in humbled fascination, I stared right back at her. She was without a doubt the most beautiful, perfect, and peaceful little creature that I had ever seen. Her perfectly groomed bright copper colored coat was so vibrant, her big brown beautiful eyes were captivating, and oh, those adorable ears! The quizzical little looks she gave me and her tentative movements told me that I was likely the first person she had ever come across, and I wanted to make a good first impression. I turned off the mower and sat quietly watching her play for more than half an hour. She quickly realized that I meant her no harm and I was enjoying every moment and feeling so blessed by her presence. What an honor — this dainty unassuming little creature had allowed me a glimpse into her tiny new world, which was my own backyard.

A little time had passed, and again there was that feeling that I was being watched. They appeared quickly and quietly out of nowhere, this beautiful little baby's momma and daddy. They stood there silently on top of the ridge at the edge of the meadow, somewhat hidden in the trees. They were watching *me* — watching *her*. It was an exciting and incredible experience! Soon, she scampered up the hill to her waiting parents. Momma gave her a quick kiss on top of her little head, and she turned back for one last look at me. Then all three disappeared, as quietly as they had appeared, back into the forest. I could hardly wait for our next chance meeting, which would happen three days later ...

"Grant me, that I see You, O Lord, reflected in the eyes of all creatures,

great and small ... and that I never forget that it is

Your love alone, that is beating in their hearts ..."

 Amen

You, watching me ...

Them, watching me, watching you ...

Your beautiful Momma ...

Big Sister ...

"Spring is God's way of saying ...

'One more time.'"

(Robert Orben)

Daddy ...

... And adorable
You!

OUR STORY ... AND SO IT GOES ...

I was completely taken by *you* and drawn in to *your* world. Everyday, I would peer out my back windows and venture out to see if you were in my meadow again, and for three wonderful weeks, I watched you learn, play, and grow stronger. I would sit discreetly by the apple tree and speak to you softly. I introduced myself and told you that you were welcome to live in my backyard and that I would try to watch over you. I assured you that you would be safe if you would stay close by and I tried my best to warn you of the dangers in the forest. I really believe that you were listening by the way you looked into my eyes. You would tilt your tiny head and your adorable oversized ears would flutter and twitch at every word. I could tell you trusted me and we were becoming friends.

Then one day, as I watched you playing, imagine my astonishment and utter surprise when all of a sudden from out of the bushes sprang another beautiful, identical, baby fawn—your sister! Twins! How lucky was I? I had not only one fawn but *two* fawns living and growing up in *my* own backyard. I could have only dreamed for something as wonderful as this to happen.

I quickly learned your habits and knew exactly where I could find you. You would either be napping on the upper ridge of the meadow with your momma and yearling sister ... nestled in under the tall pine trees ... or tucked in safely at the old wooden corner post at the West end of the meadow. The latter place, at the corner post, seemed to be your favorite napping spot because most days, that was where I could find you. There were days I would go out there and not see you right away, perhaps you were growing accustomed to my voice, because when I would call out to you "babies," you both would come running from your hiding spots. Always, I could find your momma and yearling sister a short distance away, usually resting under the trees but also keeping a watchful eye on you both. I couldn't help but feel that they felt I was "safe enough" for you to be around.

... And, I so loved your company!

"Our primary purpose in this life should be to help others ...

And if you cannot help them, at least don't hurt them."

(Dalai Lama ♥)

2

Twins!

You
and your
twin sister...

4

"And now these three remain ... faith, hope and love ...

But the greatest of these is love ..." ♡

(1 Corinthians 13:13 NIV)

5

Watching me from the safety of
the tall grass in the meadow ...

Napping at the corner post ...

Momma and daddy were always close by ...

You were so perfect ...

"And although, you neither know how to spin or weave, God dresses you and your children, for the Creator loves you greatly, and He dresses you abundantly, therefore, always seek to praise God."

(Saint Francis of Assisi)

JULY

On a sunny, quiet Sunday afternoon in late July, toting a bucket of apples and corn, I had wandered out to the meadow looking for you. I caught a glimpse of your adorably enormous, rusty colored ears just above the tall grass, which had begun to turn a late summer brown. But something wasn't quite right. You didn't pop out to greet me. You weren't running and leaping around as you normally did—you were limping! Limping badly!! *"Oh dear God,"* I thought out loud and my heart sank. Over the years, I had seen so many deer in the area with broken legs and had witnessed how difficult it was for them to heal and survive. I was devastated to think you had been hurt. What could have happened??

Wistfully I watched you limp away through the tall grass of the meadow, and up and over the hill with your sister. I desperately wanted to follow you ... with a deep sadness in my heart, I made my way back towards the house, worrying and wondering what had happened to you? ... What could I do? .. And how would I help you?

I heard you crying in the forest later that evening. The cries of a fawn in distress are heart-breaking, and were coming from the direction where I last saw you headed. I ventured out past the meadow through the tall pines to try to find you and see if there was anything I could do for you. Your momma and daddy must have heard your cries too, as we all ended up there at the exact same time. You were bedded down in the tall grass, now surrounded by your family. I still didn't know for sure what had happened to you, I just knew you were hurting. I thought perhaps it was best to let your momma and daddy take care of you. Heartbroken and feeling completely helpless, I retreated back to the house. Although I continued to look for you, every hour of every day... it would be two long days before I would see you again.

When you finally made another appearance, I could see clearly that it was so much more serious than a *broken leg*. You had suffered severe trauma to your left hind leg. The fact is your entire lower extremity and hoof were missing and I could see where you had been bleeding from your thigh, leg and nose ... It was apparent you had been caught in a foot-trap and were in need of more help than I could ever provide. Who would do such a thing to you? And how would you survive with only three tiny legs in a forest full of dangers? Reflected in your eyes, I could see you had surrendered to your injury and had adopted a new *crooked little walk*. It was heart wrenching to watch. Your cries in the forest were unbearable. Immediately I set out to try to find you professional help. I felt your injuries were life threatening and you needed critical care—now!

In the hours and days that followed, I searched and searched and made phone call after phone call, trying to find someone, *anyone*, who could help me rescue you. I tried every veterinarian and wildlife rehabber I could find. Every time, I would hit a dead end. It was so far beyond discouraging. I was advised to put the antibiotic Tetracycline in your water supply to try to ward off any infections. That's when I decided to name you "Hope" because, each day as night would fall, I hoped and prayed that you could somehow survive the perils of a dark forest.

You were limping, limping badly!!

You disappeared up and over the hill ...

~

"You never know how strong you are ... until being strong is the only choice you have."

(unknown)

I decided to name you "Hope" ...

... because I hoped you could survive
this cruel old world ...

"And if we dare to look into those beautiful eyes, then we shall feel their
suffering ... in our hearts."

(Jane Goodall)

13

"Out of suffering, have emerged the strongest souls♥ the most massive characters, are seared with scars."

(Kahlil Gibran)

FOR EIGHTEEN WEEKS...

I searched for someone with enough compassion to want to help you. Although I did every-thing I could think of, the bitter reality was that no help was coming. With each new lead was another frustrating roadblock. So for the next eighteen weeks, my days and evenings revolved around you, sweet Hope, and your needs. *You* became my priority. It would be up to me to care for and comfort you, and I would do my best.

Each day, I would sit and wait for you behind the apple tree with corn and apples, and soon you started coming closer to the house, looking and waiting for me too! I fed you and watered you by day and prayed for and worried over you as night fell. I hardly noticed that Spring had turned into Summer. The days were long and hot. Some days, I would find you covered in cockle burrs, probably from a tumble down the hill.

"Our greatest glory is not in never falling, but in rising, every time we fall."
(Ralph Waldo Emerson)

And other days, you would show up beat down and bleeding. God only knew the hardships that befell you the night before. Running from the coyotes, dodging scrapped barbed wire, fences and cars or just navigating the slippery rocky ridges and cliffs of the forest in the darkness. Despite it all, with humble determination, you fought your battles, one after another ... you were such a brave little girl...

Still, your momma, daddy, and sisters were usually close by. We all did our best to look after you. Sister would stay with you for afternoon naps, and evenings I could find you, your sisters, and momma under the big apple tree. Your beautiful momma would be nuzzling you and gently pulling the burrs from your fur, cleaning your ears, and kissing you softly on your precious little face. Your daddy would stand watch and you all just carried on ...

You had all accepted your fate ... I had not ...

And spring ....

... evolved into Summer.

The days were long and hot ...

17

Momma was teaching you how
to forage for food ...

... and she loved you so much.

WATCHING... WAITING ...

Early mornings, I would watch out my window and wait for you to appear. Many mornings, you would show up, thirsty and famished from your nights' journey and trials. Most afternoons, you would wander down to the patio, looking for me! You trusted me and that was the best feeling. I would always breathe a sigh of relief when I would finally see you, thanking God that you had made it safely through another night. Some nights, I would hear the terrifying howls of the coyotes. I would lie in my bed and pray for your protection.

I was always comforted by your quiet, calming presence... After our visits I would stand and watch your heart wrenching, little *side-winding walk* as you headed back to the forest. There was no more scampering away. Just standing to eat was difficult, you would try to stretch down your little leg, reaching for the ground for balance with a little hoof that was no longer there. I found it easier on you if I would set your food beside the tree and you could lean into it while you ate. Although it wasn't that far, just getting from one edge of the meadow to the other was exhausting and quite a feat for you. Your back was beginning to

"Courage doesn't always roar ... Sometimes courage is the quiet voice, at the end of the day that says, 'I'll try again, tomorrow.'"

(Mary Anne Radamacher)

bow and your front shoulder was becoming misshapen from always having to lean on it ... In such a short time your perfect little body had become so crooked and twisted. You were given no choice—your spirit and determination always pushed you forward. You just *did* what you needed to *do* the best you could to get by. I would find myself talking to God a lot in those days, asking Him to *help me ... help you* and wondering, *"Why?" Why* did this have to happen to you? Something so precious ... so gentle ... so sweet ... *Why??* My faith in God is very strong, and I trust Him in all things ... I didn't blame Him for your injury I just didn't understand it. It's very difficult to watch such suffering of the innocent and feel so helpless. Life in the forest was not easy...

"Sometimes ... even to live, is an act of courage."

(Seneca)

Every single day ... was a

struggle survive ...

... with another battle to fight. ...

You tried and tried so hard and you NEVER, ever gave up...

"Dare to reach out your hand, into the darkness,

to pull another hand, into the Light."

(Amrie Desai)

Summer day in the flowers under momma's
watchful eye, from a distance ...

25

"Be faithful in small things, because it is in them that your strength lies."

(Mother Teresa)

AUTUMN

The dark green leaves began to turn colors of warm gold and red. The rose hips were appearing; the geese were regrouping to fly south; and all the "Spring babes"—the cottontail rabbits, the quail, the robins, and the squirrels—had all grown up and were on their own. Summer was somehow losing its way and transforming itself into Fall. Your coat was changing color too, from the bright and beautiful rusty red to a light tannish gray. You were losing your bright little white speckles ... You too were growing up ... against the odds. Your family began leaving you alone or with me for longer periods of time, as they began their Fall migration around the forest and hills. Each day was such an ordeal for you and brought with it new obstacles to overcome.

... In spite of it all, you never, ever gave up!

Your telltale little crooked walk announced to the world that you were the "weak link" of the herd. The other deer from the other local herds, the 'bullies', would come and try to push you around and away from the food and fresh water that I had sat out for *you* ... So I began sitting with you while you ate each morning and each evening, so you could get your tummy full. I'd toss apples and pears at them to keep them at bay, sometimes your daddy would wander in and chase them off, so you could eat in peace. Occasionally, your momma would see you struggling too, and she would come running and stomping—'Momma to the rescue'. She'd guard you and gently kiss you. We all knew you needed the nourishment more than the others did, so you would have enough energy and strength just to get through the long, hard days and nights that awaited you.

'Do not lose hope ... when the sun goes down, the stars come out'

(unknown)

You tried so hard to use a little hoof ...

that just wasn't there ...

~

"I do not at all, understand the mystery of Grace ... only that it meets us where we are ... but does not leave us where it found us."

(Anne Lamott)

Somehow ... Summer loses its way and is transformed into Fall ...

'Momma to the rescue' ...

There is no love like a
Mothers' love ♡

When the bullies come,
and they do come, I'll be right
there to protect you ...

"Apples at sunset" ...

OCTOBER CAME AND WENT ...

November rains began to fall. My heart broke time and time again, as I would watch you slip and slide and sometimes fall. You'd be covered in mud, but you'd pick yourself right back up, and you would be on your way. The harshness of your life was beginning to show on your drawn, little face, and each day, new lumps or bumps would appear, telling of the arduous night you had had. I desperately wanted to scoop you up into my arms and keep you safe and watch over you forever ... However, I had been sternly admonished, not to do that ...

I hope you know that I tried everything I could think of to protect and defend you and to try to get you the professional care you *needed*, the care you *deserved*. There was just no help to be found, and for that, my courageous little warrior ... I am so sorry ...

"You were given this life, because you were strong enough to live it ..."

(Nishan Panwar)

"Pain and suffering have come into your life, but remember pain, sorrow and suffering are but the kiss of Jesus..."

"... a sign that you have come so close to Him, that He can kiss you."

(Mother Teresa)

FALLING SNOW...

The first light snowfall came just a week or so before Thanksgiving. I was dreading Winter coming. I knew how difficult ice and snow would make it for you to get around. I woke up early one morning to your little crooked trail in the new fallen snow. It lead from the forest down to my patio ... I cried, as I stood there looking at it ...

It seemed so profound ...

There in the skiff of snow in my backyard was the story of your life—"Hope's Trail". It showed how the simplest pathway for all the others was like climbing the tallest mountain for you. It was the fate you were dealt, and undaunted, you did your best with such grace, courage, dignity, and perseverance ... You were so brave and I was so proud of you ...

Your sad story makes grown men cry ...

37

"Courage is not having the strength to go on.
Courage is going on, when you don't
have the strength."
(Theodore Roosevelt)

Sunday afternoon ...

November 18th ...

... the last photos
I have of Hope ...

40

A VERY SAD NOVEMBER

One cool, blustery day in late November, I sat quietly behind the apple tree with you as you ate. After getting your fill of alfalfa, corn, pears, apples, and water, the sun was beginning to settle in the chilly Western sky. Like every evening before, I knew you'd be tucking yourself in for the night. It had become your routine to wander up under the safety of the tall pine trees, with the low sweeping boughs, behind the house and bed down. So I headed back towards the house ...

For some reason, I turned back to watch you go. You had changed directions ... Maybe it was because your sister had returned and was wandering back through the yard. Whatever the reason, I watched you follow her down the trail that led back to the forest. I had watched you do that a hundred times before, but this time just felt different. I didn't know why it did—it just did.

I called out your name, and you turned and looked back at me for just a moment. Your sister was getting too far ahead of you, so away you turned and quickly followed after her.

Both you and your sister disappeared into the forest ...

Gone from my field of vision ... Gone with the last light of the day ...

... *Just gone* ...

I didn't know at the time that this would be the very last time I would see you, but it was ...

... you followed your sister ...

... you both disappeared

into the forest ...

♡

... Gone from my

field of vision ...

... Gone with the last

light of day ...

... Just gone ...

43

"How lucky I am, to have something, that makes saying goodbye ... so hard."

(A.A. Milne, "Winnie The Pooh")

"His Eye is on The Sparrow"

(Martin and Gabriel, 1905)

"Hope is Faith, holding out its hand in the darkness..."
(George Iles)

DEAR HOPE,

I am so sorry that I couldn't shield you from all the dangers of the forest. I am so sorry that we all failed you. I would have done anything for you, anything to protect you. I hope you knew that I tried my best. I only wish there was something more I could have done ...

Perhaps God answered my prayers—not in the manner that I had hoped He would, but He answered them just the same and in the manner that was best for you. I believe that His heart broke right along with mine as He watched you battling and struggling to survive. You had had enough, and on that dark, cold wintery night ... He called you *Home*.

Oh, how I missed you ... your precious little face and your quiet, peaceful presence ... Every morning and every afternoon, I would catch myself looking out the window for you, as I had done daily for the past twenty-one weeks. I couldn't believe that you were really gone. You were a ray of sunshine in a harsh and unkind world ....

... And so it continues, the story of *you* and *your* journey... that has now become *my* journey. A story of 'Hope'... hope for the others that will follow you ....

46

EPILOGUE

'Run free, sweet baby ... You are truly 'free' now ...'

... Godspeed ♡

... After losing Hope and discovering at the edge of the forest what had been left of my beautiful, broken baby, I was shattered ... As I stood on the ridge above the meadow, staring down in disbelief at the devastation below, I was overcome with the deepest sadness. This once magical enchanting place, 'the forest', had become so cold, so dark and so ugly, overnight ... I stumbled down to where she lay, and I sat and cried amidst what remained of this delicate, loving creature. I wept for her and her torn up little body ... I wept for her family, for myself and our heartbreaking loss. My heartache was inconsolable. I could barely breathe, I felt like someone had reached in and torn my heart right from my chest. I stood up and tried, but couldn't compose myself. I really couldn't even move... I kneeled back down to where what was left of her lay ... My mind was racing and

turned again to thoughts of her beautiful momma, sisters and daddy... Oh my God, what were they thinking and feeling? Did they know? Did they see it happen? Were they hurt, trying to save her or trying to help her escape? Were they so frightened and traumatized by what had happened that I would never see them again, as well? I had to stop thinking or I'd lose my mind ...

Somehow, I made it back home and found myself driving down to the corner store ... Luckily, I didn't run into anyone I knew while there because I was a mess. I went straight to the flower shop and there, at the entrance, was a gorgeous bouquet of eighteen long-stemmed pink roses ... Although I had not known exactly what I was looking for, when I entered the store, they were exactly what I wanted ... It was as if they had been placed there with purpose ... so I bought them and headed back home and back to the scene of the unspeakable crime ...

I took six of the roses and laid them on her "grave"—one for her ... one for her momma ... one for each of her sisters ... one for her daddy... and one for me. I took the remaining twelve roses and began tearing the petals off of them, scattering them over the "area" in which I had found her. Afterwards, I sat on a rock nearby ... My tears continued to silently fall ... I hoped and prayed that her death was "quick and painless" for her sake, as she had already endured too much pain and suffering in her short little life.

As I sat there heartbroken and grieving, I began to hear some rustling in the trees and bushes behind me and up over my left shoulder. I sat waiting and watching to see "who" or "what" it might be. The sun was just beginning to set as I thought to myself, "Here I am, all alone in the darkening and dangerous forest ... maybe I shouldn't be" ... When suddenly, the sources of the rustling quietly appeared. Standing there majestically and loyally on the ridge above me was Hope's momma, twin sister, and yearling sister. Had they come to help me say goodbye to "our" tiny sweetheart? ... Whatever the reason, I felt so honored and blessed to be in their company once more.

It was then and there that I made my promise to all of them and myself that I would try to make a difference—try to make something good out of something so terrible ...

"'FAITH' ... is seeing Light, with your heart,

when all your eyes see, is darkness."

(Unknown)

... 'And Winter came', delivering a beautiful, bright white new snowfall 'to lift my spirits', bringing a lightness to my sadness and a peace to my heart. It blanketed the dark and somber sacred ground of the forest ...

All Winter long, Hope's mom and dad and sisters came to call regularly. I was so comforted that her family was still coming around and visiting me. We now had an extraordinary bond. We had all lost someone so very, very dear to our hearts ... It was healing for me to see them still wandering in and out of the yard ...

'AND WINTER MELTED INTO SPRING'

All I knew was that I couldn't look at my meadow or apple tree and not think about her. The bittersweet memory of Hope was everywhere I turned ... I couldn't believe how this unassuming little being had embedded herself so deeply into my soul ...

The robins reappeared and sunny days were returning. One day I was outside, refreshing the deer water and throwing out some corn and the last of the winter alfalfa when from out of the forest, Hope's dad appeared—missing one antler.

It's curious how you get to know each of the deer by their markings ... or their ear shapes ... or their distinct eyes and eyebrows ... their tails, their scars, and their antlers.

I saw him standing there, with the one antler he had left that distinguished him from the rest of them. It almost saddened me. He looked very much like all the other bucks who wander in and out of the yard all year long. Only his antlers told me he was Hope's daddy. I looked at him and spoke softly to him. He held his head a little cocked, the way Hope used to when I would speak to her (I supposed it was partly because of the imbalance of only having one large antler on his head).

Either way, I tried to explain to him that once he would shed his other antler, I probably wouldn't recognize him anymore, that it was the uniqueness of his drop-tine antler that I knew him by. I casually pointed out to him, that maybe he could shed it here in my backyard so I could keep it to remember him by. He went about his grazing, I finished what I was doing, and wandered back to the house ...

The next morning I ventured outside, as I always did to air the dogs, I couldn't believe my eyes, right there, at the edge of the tree line, sticking straight into the ground was his antler—the very antler I had hoped to have as a keepsake someday! I thought to myself, "Oh my gosh! He really did leave it here for me" ... This "family" that I had adopted had also adopted me ... and I was honored to have their companionship and trust.

Initially, I was dreading Spring this year. I kept seeing all the momma does' bellies growing larger as they were preparing to have their babies. I thought to myself ... I just can't watch. With the tragic loss of Hope so freshly burned into my memory and etched into my heart and soul, I reflected, 'I cannot bear to get attached and be hurt again by the inevitable injuries that befall them. I won't wander the meadow ... I won't watch out the window ... I won't fall in love with those beautiful little speckled darlings ... I won't ... I won't ...'

Well ... I have and I am. I have been watching seven of the most beautiful babies, running, leaping, growing, playing and resting in my yard, and meadow. I have watched them go from being glued to their mommas' sides to venturing out on their own into this big new world before them. Growing up! 'New life has begun once again' in my meadow, in "Hope's Meadow" ... and my heart is full and I am so grateful for the experience.

Hope's momma has two adorable brand new babies, her twin sister has one darling new baby, Hope's big sister, the yearling from last year, also has two new babies, and two other does, are raising their babies in 'our' meadow. How lucky am I? I not only have one new baby but seven! I have already promised them the same things I had promised Hope and her sister: as long as they stay close by to my backyard, I will love them, feed and water them, and do my best to protect them ...

I decided to visit Hope's grave one last time to tell her about the new babies and let her know that I still think about her ... that I will always think about her.

And lying neatly on her grave, as if placed there on purpose, were two brand new antler sheds ...

It appears that I am not her only visitor ....

My gift ...

Always together ...

POSTSCRIPT

"You have not lived, until you have done something for someone,

who can never repay you."

(Anonymous)

I quickly learned that it wasn't just me that Hope's magic had touched but all of my family and friends who came to know her through social media and my writings and photos. They were also captivated and enchanted by her. I received so many encouraging and sympathetic messages at her passing. Not only was *I* mourning and sad at the tragic heart-rending death of a very special fawn, I learned that many, many tears were being shed across the country for this painful loss of such sweet innocence … *Our* Hope …

... Over a year has passed, and I still cry for her ... My heart still hurts ... My 'wound' still has not yet healed ...

One quote that I have found to be quite poignant for me is:

"The wound is the place, where the Light enters you."

(Rumi)

My wound was my heart. Hope was my Light ... a Light to many of us.

Looking back ... were I to know how it all would end, would I have let myself become so attached? ... So invested? Absolutely, I would! Would I have looked the other way? ... Would I have spared myself the sight of such terrible suffering? No, absolutely I would not have! Although that was one of the most heartbreaking Summers and Falls of my life, my bond with Hope has truly been one of the greatest joys of my life. Her life story has changed me in ways I find difficult to put into words ... Despite unspeakable adversity, her inspiration, her grace, her quiet strength, and unforgettable presence, has challenged me, to try and make a difference in the innocent lives of those who suffer ... those without a voice ...

... As the old song goes, "And now, I'm glad I didn't know, the way it all would end, the way it all would go ... Our lives, are better left to chance, I could have missed the pain ... but I'd of had to miss ... the *Dance* ..." ~ *Garth Brooks, "The Dance"*

... I wouldn't have missed this for the world ...

Hope's memory
will live on ...

57

"May every Sunrise bring you Hope ... May every Sunset bring you Peace"

(Unknown)

"... This world was never meant for one, as beautiful ... as you."

"Starry, Starry Night (Vincent)" – Don McLean

58

In Memory of an extraordinary, beautiful baby fawn named Hope

~

November Rain

(by Sister Laura Michels, Gonzaga University)

November Rain, like a quiet kind of crying,

Dulls the walkways, with clumps of dampened leaves ...

I think, "O God, You created this season, to test our faith" ...

In Your love, You will soon send a snowfall,

That brings a brightness to lift our Spirit ...

Our faith invites us to remember,

That Winter melts its way into Spring,

And a new life, begins ... once again ...

♡

... the sun still rises in the East,

and darkness falls at night,

nothing now seems quite the same,

each day is not so bright ...

the birds still sing,

the flowers grow,

and the breeze still whispers, too ...

but it will never, ever be,

the same world, without you ...

it's so sad you had to go away,

your leaving caused such pain ...

but you were Very Special,

and Earth's loss,

is Heavens' gain ...

(unknown)

"Where flowers bloom ... so does hope"

(Lady Bird Johnson)

May 2013

(the corner post in the top far right, was Hope's favorite napping spot ...)

"Hope's Meadow"... one lone wild iris grows ...

Momma, resting in the meadow ...

May 2013

'... And a new life begins
... Once again ...'

...Godspeed babies...

June 2013

The story of

'Hope' ...

... The circle, complete ...

In Memory of the Innocent ...

... taken much too soon 2013 - 2014

faith ...

grace ...

baby buck ...

little Winter baby ...

Working on Hope's story, has truly been a labor of love, for me ... In my attempt to keep my promise and honor her life and her struggle to survive, the proceeds of this book will go towards my dream of building 'Hope's Trail Rescue and Sanctuary' in Eastern Washington ... a safe haven for injured or orphaned fawns ...

Every year, many viable fawns are euthanized unnecessarily and often times, inhumanely, because their moms may have been hit by a car, leaving them orphaned ... perhaps they, themselves have been injured ... or because people have taken them from their 'hiding spots', believing they were abandoned, when in reality, they have NOT been. Their mothers tuck them away and leave them alone, for their protection from predators, returning only to feed them. At the rescue, these fawns would now have a safe place to rehab and grow, and when ready, released back into the wild ...

... For more information on how you can become a part of 'Hope's Trail Rescue and Sanctuary', please go to our website at www.atrailofhope.com

... Or you can follow us on Facebook at www.facebook.com/a.trail.of.hope

... Or you may e-mail me directly at msfish1962@gmail.com

CPSIA information can be obtained
at www.ICGtesting.com
Printed in the USA
BVXC01n1109290914
368073BV00003B/6